The Gospel According to Ma

Compiled by:
Brian Edwards (Imani)

Design & layout:
Brian Edwards (Imani)

Published 2013 by:
JKB Independent Publishers
United Kingdom

Copyright © 2013 Brian Edwards

All Rights Reserved:
No section of this book should be reproduced or copied in any form or stored in a retrieval system without the express consent of the Publisher.

ISBN-13: 978-1494376369
ISBN-10: 1494376369

Contents

	PAGES
Preface & Introduction	(4 - 5)
CHAPTER (1) CONCEPT OF GOD	(6 - 8)

1. Who or What is God
2. The Limitless Power of Almighty God & mankind's limit of power
3. Purpose of Creation
4. The Image of God
5. The Trinity
6. What is the Holy Ghost
7. No one but you can save your soul

CHAPTER (2) ON RELIGION	(9 - 11)

8. What is Religion
9. Man's religion
10. Righteousness
11. Masters of your own Destiny
12. Mind, Body and Soul
13. Preserve your Soul

CHAPTER (3) ON THE CHRIST   PAGES (12 - 17)

14. The Doctrine of Christ
15. Christ & Christianity
16. Christ the greatest reformer
17. Christ the Example
18. Living the Life of Christ
19. Christ's Doctrine rejected by the Classes
20. The Character of Man
21. Christianity a Moving Force

CHAPTER (4) MANKIND & CHRIST   (17 - 23)

22. Man's Kinship With His Creator
23. The Selfishness of Mankind
24. Christ is for All, so we are for All
25. Christ Taught Love
26. Let us Live Like Christ both in body & spirit
27. Christ never corrupted his Soul
28. God Not Interested in the Physical Activities of Man
29. The Spirit of God and the Mission of Christ
30. The Sign of the Cross

Appendix:
(Poem) - Christ the Way   (24)
(Prayer) - My Altar   (25)

"If Christ as man never existed, but was only an assumption, it would have been a glorious assumption to set man a high spiritual example of how he should live".

PREFACE & INTRODUCTION

The Gospel According to Marcus Garvey, is a small booklet containing 30 speeches or words of The Rt. Honourable Marcus Garvey that explore some of is teachings, idea's, philosophies and opinions in regards to and specifically relating to God, The Christ, Religion and their role or place in the African Liberation Struggle. Although countless of millions of Black people today and in the past have adhered strictly to Garvey's political and economic views and advice, few have been as interested or even aware of his religious and spiritual views. Notwithstanding the fact that many even revere him as a prophet sent by God Almighty to redeem the Black race. As a prophet or messenger, one would expect people to be interested in what or which God he himself worshipped.
Not only should this information be of the utmost importance, but should not this be, the foundation upon which people who proclaim to be following him and revere him as a prophet, themselves focus their worship. Nevertheless Garvey's legacy has become a type of religion unto itself, in the form of Garveyism, with adherents calling themselves Garveyite's.

These Garveyite's professing Garveyism can be found within all and every religion, political, community or cultural group and organisation, where black people are found working towards tackling issues affecting Black communities all over the modern world. Therefore Garveyism today supersedes all religions or concepts impacting on black African people. As whether a person professes to be a Black Muslim, Christian, Rasta, Hebrew Israelite, Black Panther, Pan-Africanist, Black Nationalist, African Spiritualist, democrat or republican, conservative or labourite or has any other allegiance, as long as they profess also to have a desire to truly help change the circumstances of black people, most of them still consider themselves and profess themselves to be Garveyite's, so their are Muslim Garveyites, Christian Garveyites, African Spiritualist Garveyites and so on. This is very important to note as this phenomena is not afforded any other Black personality, making Garvey one of the few people or entities that could potentially unite the currently very much disunited Black nation.

Like most religious icons in history, such as Buddha, Mohammad, Guru Nanak and Jesus, Garvey's followers have drifted far from what he taught resulting in them like most other modern day religious adherents not living the life advised and therefore baring no actual fruits, The editor is of the opinion that to be a Garveyite one must be aware of what Garvey instructs, and to help accomplished the task assigned them by their leader, they must try to draw from the same inspiration that inspired Garvey himself. This booklet has been created to help Garveyites better understand what Garvey's views were in regards to the accepted and advised faith black people should follow. Although many will chose not to adhere to these teachings for what ever reason, it is proposed that unless one does they can not truly be a Garveyite, or even overstand Garvey, his mission and African history, culture and ancient heritage.

It is important to note that although outlined here are many of Garvey's views in his analysis of the western view of God, Christ & Religion as he found it, his opinions although contradictory to much western dogma, it is inline with some of the most ancient ideas of God, held by African people as well as today by many modern African Traditionalist.

So let us, as Garvey instructs,
"see everything through the spectacles of Ethiopia".
(Imani 2013)

ON THE CONCEPT OF GOD

1. WHO OR WHAT IS GOD

"There is a God and we believe in Him. He is not a person nor a physical being. He is spirit and He is universal intelligence. *Never deny that there is a God.* God being universal intelligence created the universe out of that intelligence. It is intelligence that creates.
Man is a part of the creation of universal intelligence and man was created in the image and likeness of God only by his intelligence. It is the intelligence of man that is like God, but man's intelligence is only a unitary particle of God's universal intelligence".

2. THE LIMITLESS POWER OF GOD & MANKIND'S LIMIT OF POWER

"God out of His universal intelligence made matter and made mind. That matter is made by God and man is matter as well as mind; then man must be in the image of God, because nothing could exist without God. As God made the universe out of His universal knowledge or intelligence so man in his unitary knowledge or intelligence can make a typewriter, an automobile or a chair, but cannot make the universe because his unitary intelligence is not as much or as great as universal intelligence. All the unitary intelligence of the universe goes to make God who is the embodiment of all intelligence, so no man can be as great as God because he is only a unit of God and God is the whole".

3. PURPOSE OF CREATION

"God Almighty created each and every one of us for a place in the world, and for the least of us to think that we were created only to be what we are and not what we can make ourselves, is to impute an improper motive to the Creator for creating us."

4. THE IMAGE OF GOD

"If the white man has the idea of a white God, let him worship his God as he desires. If the yellow man's God is of his race let him worship his God as he sees fit. We, as Negroes, have found a new ideal. Whilst our God has no colour, yet it is human to see everything through one's own spectacles, and since the white people have seen their God through white spectacles, we only now started out, late though it be, to see our God through our own spectacles. The God of Isaac and the God of Jacob. We Negroes believe in the God of Ethiopia, the everlasting God - God the Father, God the Son and God the Holy Ghost, the One God of all ages. That is the God in whom we believe, but we shall worship Him through the spectacles of Ethiopia."

5. THE TRINITY

"The *DOCTRINE OF THE TRINITY OF GOD, THE FATHER, THE SON AND THE HOLY GHOST*, is not commonly understood by the ordinary mind that will not think in the guiding spirit of God.
To the mind that thinks with the spirit of God it is very pleasingly under- stood that the Godhead is one in three parts; all related and all doing good. You cannot separate them. This may be a mystery which the ordinary intelligence of man cannot explain because man is not God in intelligence, but nevertheless, it explains the riddle of the universe. It is preposterous for man to say that he can analyze God in his completeness because man is only a finite and small unit of Divine and Universal Intelligence. So while universal intelligence can analyze unitary intelligence, unitary intelligence cannot analyze universal intelligence.

So leave out trying to be like God by demanding from God in mental analysis; why he does what he does, and why he does not do the other thing. You are not competent. No part is greater than the whole. The whole is always greater than any single part and man is only a single part of God; so he cannot be as great in mind as God".

6. WHAT IS THE HOLY GHOST

"The Holy Ghost is the spirit of God at large. It is everywhere. It is really what we call the spirit. In everything that you see, there is the spirit of the Holy Ghost. Man can be a complete manifestation of that spirit, for as a unit in him the spirit becomes responsible and lives and acts. The Holy Ghost is the perfect spirit of God's intelligence which is distinct from matter as particles of creation. No particle can exist in nature without the knowledge of God, because God created it. A particle may not contain the spirit of the Holy Ghost.
When life is given and thought is to be expressed there we have the spirit of the Holy Ghost. A bit of iron may not have the spirit of the Holy Ghost; but in man there are the elements of iron as well as other elements, and the complete thoughtfulness of man is made up of all of these elements which give existence to the spirit of the Holy Ghost, just as all things are related and man is related to all things in nature.
So God is everywhere in nature, but the spirit of the Holy Ghost is only in the higher thought life, and the highest thought life we know is man. The Holy Ghost spirit is always in man".

7. NO ONE BUT YOU CAN SAVE YOUR SOUL

"You can worship God by yourself. You are responsible to God by yourself. You have to live your own soul before God. Nobody, but you can save your soul. Others may advise you on how to shape your soul; because of your ignorance of life. Keep in communion with God.
No one but you can save your soul; in your soul [lies] relationship with God. Therefore, always worship with your own heart, soul and mind when you want to commune with God. Make your heart, soul or mind your altar and express it in the following way". (see My Alter Prayer)

ON RELIGION

8. WHAT IS RELIGION

"Religion is one's opinion and belief in some ethical truth. To be a Christian is to have the religion of Christ, and so to be a believer of Mohammed is to be a Mohammedan (Muslim) but there are so many religions that every man seems to be a religion unto himself. No two persons think alike, even if they outwardly profess the same faith, so we have as many religions in Christianity as we have believers".

9. MAN'S RELIGION

"Man's religion is something that we cannot eliminate from his system or destroy in him; therefore, it is folly for any man to go about attacking another man's religion, because to him it is fundamental. You may be a Christian; you may be Muhammadan; that is your religion … We are all entitled to our religious beliefs. Therefore any man who gets out and attacks religions, thinking he can convert men to the Organization by so doing is not helping the Organization. He is doing it more harm than good. We have reached the point where if we are to accomplish anything whatever we should have a unison and accord. We only have to look at the other races and we find the majority stand together in one religious belief. We have found men of the white world, stand together in one belief. We have found men of the brown world standing together in one belief; the yellow people having there singular belief in that respect and this singular belief has kept them together and strengthened them". (Blackman, 08/31/1929)

10. RIGHTEOUSNESS

"...Our cause is based upon righteousness. And anything that is not righteous we have no respect for, because God Almighty is our leader and Jesus Christ our standard bearer".

11. MASTERS OF YOUR OWN DESTINY

"I repeat that God created you masters of your own destiny, masters of your own fate, and you can pay no higher tribute to your Divine Master than function as man, as He created you.
The highest compliment we can pay to our Creator; the highest respect we can pay to our risen Lord and Savior, is that of feeling that He has created us as His masterpiece; His perfect instruments of His own existence, because in us is reflected the very being of God.
When it is said that we are created in His own image, we ourselves reflect His greatness, we ourselves reflect the part of God the Father, God the Son, and God the Holy Ghost, and when we allow ourselves to be subjected and create others as our superior, we hurl an insult at our Creator who made us in the fullness of ourselves. I trust that you will so live today as to realize that you are masters of your own destiny, masters of your fate; if there is anything you want in this world it is for you to strike out with confidence and faith in self and reach for it, because God has created it for your happiness where so ever you may find it in nature. Nature is bountiful; nature is resourceful, and nature is willing to obey the command of man--Man the sovereign lord; man who is supposed to hold dominion and take possession of this great world of ours".

12. MIND, BODY AND SOUL

"There is a confusion of expression between mind, soul and heart. These expressions are used with laxity. In fact, they all mean the same thing. The soul of man is the mind of man and when we speak of the heart, not the physical thing, but the expressive thing, we mean the soul, which is the mind. So always remember that you have a body, which is the physical case for the soul, which is the mind; which is the heart in the sentimental sense of the heart expressing itself.

The spirit is greater than all and it is the Holy Ghost and God in man. The spirit advises the soul. It guides and guards the soul and when it is disgusted with the behaviour of the soul, it leaves the physical body and the physical body dies, as we describe it. In fact, the physical body does not die. It becomes matter in a different form.

It may become earth again, from which flowers and vegetation grow and bloom, and from which man eats back himself in the form of fruit and vegetable life. Nothing is lost in nature and nothing really dies, because everything is God's that is eternal and everlasting.

A good soul may pass away in what we call death, like a bad soul, but that soul also has an everlasting identity that may pass into some higher realm of usefulness. It may become an angel or it may be used by God in some higher sphere.

The wicked soul never comes back. It goes out and that is man's hell. Its going out is called, "going to hell," because it never lives again as a soul. Therefore, a good soul lives forever. A bad soul passes out when the spirit of God has left the body in which the soul is found. The soul is judged before it completely disappears, and will recognize its punishment in the judgment before God. Then it is completely obliterated".

13. PRESERVE YOUR SOUL

"When it is said, "Thou shalt not kill," it is meant thou shall not kill the soul; because the soul is the personality of man. "Thou shall not kill," does not refer to the flesh because flesh is matter, and matter passes from one stage to another. By change, it is always matter, but if the soul does wickedness and evil, it dies. It only lives when it is perfect in keeping with God's goodness. Therefore, when it is said "Thou shall not kill," it means you must not kill the soul of man.
This is how warriors such as Napoleon, the Emperors, Pharaohs and the old religious warriors who fought battles among men interpreted it. This is how the Israelites interpreted it when they fought against the Philistines. This is how Joshua interpreted it when he fought against the Canaanites. This is how it shall ever be because man shall ever be at war with man in the fight of good against evil".

ON THE CHRIST

14. THE DOCTRINE OF CHRIST

"The doctrine of God carries with it the belief in the Father, Son and Holy Ghost. Christ is supposed to be the begotten Son of God. He had a special mission and that was to take on the form of man, to teach man how to lift himself back to God. For that reason Christ was born as man and came to the world.
If Christ as man never existed, but was only an assumption, it would have been a glorious assumption to set man a high spiritual example of how he should live.

There is no cause to doubt that Christ lived. Because you did not see him and feel him yourself as Thomas did, why should you doubt his existence? If you can doubt that, you may as well doubt that your great grandfather ever lived; because you never saw him nor touched him. Logically, there is fair assumption for you to believe that your grandfather whom you knew must have had a father in order to have been born. Logically, his father must have been your great grandfather. You don't have to see everything to believe it. You must trust some things to those who lived before you. You have good reason to believe that somebody or something existed before you came here. Never doubt that Christ lived; never doubt that God lived because great things happened to prove that before you came into the world. Deny that positively which you know of, and not that which you do not know of".

15. CHRIST & CHRISTIANITY

"A form of religion practised by the millions, but as mis-understood, and unreal to the majority as gravitation is to the untutored savage. We profess to live in the atmosphere of Christianity, yet our acts are as barbarous as if we never knew Christ. He taught us to love, yet we hate; to forgive, yet we revenge; to be merciful, yet we condemn and punish, and still we are Christians.
If hell is what we are taught it is, then there will be more Christians there than days in all creation. To be a true Christian one must be like Christ and practice Christianity, not as the Bishop does, but as he says, for if our lives were to be patterned after the other fellow's all of us, Bishop, Priest and Layman would ultimately meet around the furnace of hell, and none of us, because of our sins, would see salvation".

16. CHRIST THE GREATEST REFORMER

"When man had fallen in sin from his spiritual kinship to his Creator and disgust reigned even in heaven among the angels and 'the Holy One, who brought out of chaos the great universe, there sprang up divine sympathy, divine love—a sympathy and love within the Trinity caused, the Son of God to vouchsafe Himself as the Redeemer of mankind, as the Redeemer of the world.

He betook to Himself, with the authority of His Father, the duty, the work, the labour, the sacrifice, to bring man nearer to his Creator, to bring man back to his God.

The angels on that first Christmas morn notified the world that the Christ was to be born. He did not of Himself come down in His spiritual image from the heaven on high, but for the purpose of drawing Himself nearer man He took on the flesh and was born of a virgin woman, and in that stable at Bethlehem; the whole world, through the message of the angels, was told of the great happening and men journeyed from far and near to see the Christ. To some, His birth was a disappointment, because He was born lowly; He was born amid poor conditions and circumstances; He was not born of the reigning household; He was born only of a carpenter, an humble labourer, and therefore to many His birth was a disappointment.

The prophets foretold the birth of Christ; the prophets foretold the birth of the Redeemer, and men were looking for Him everywhere. The race to which he was to be born expected a redeemer in pomp and glory, and when He came in a manger they were disappointed; they were disgusted and they denied Him as the Christ. They said He was not the Christ; He was not the Promised One; He was not the Son of God; He was an impostor; but others who had faith believed that He was the Christ. And the lowly babe that was born to us in the sinful world 1922 years ago grew up amidst the surroundings of prejudice, amidst the surroundings of disgust and dissatisfaction to take on His work, to perform His labour as the Christ, as the redeemer of man, as the redeemer of the world".

17. CHRIST THE EXAMPLE

"Christ as a Living Example to Man, the man who took on flesh, physical as ours, moved among us even as we go about our daily business and occupation today. They could not believe that He was the Son of God. but in Him there was that which no man knew, which no man had; in Him was a spotless soul, was a spotless character never yet known to the world beyond the Christ in all God's creation.
There never came into the world a character like Jesus, pure, spotless, immaculate, divine like unto God, as God would have each of us to be. When God created man and breathed into his nostrils the breath of life, when God gave to man a living soul, God expected that man would live the spiritual life of the Christ, and when man sinned, when man fell from grace. God became disgusted, God became dissatisfied. If we could see the sufferings of Christ, if we could see the patience of Christ, if we could see the very crucifixion of Christ, then we would see the creature, the being spiritual that God would have us be; and knowing ourselves as we do, we could well realize how far we are from God".

18. LIVING THE LIFE OF CHRIST

"For man to see his God, for man to face His judgment and become one of the elect of the High Divine, of the Holy One, is for man to live the life of the Christ—the spotless life, the holy life, the life without sin, and that is a journey that every one in the Christian world is called upon to make. If we cannot make it, we cannot expect to see our God. Man has fallen so low, man has fallen so far from his high estate, as created and given him by God, that even now man does not know himself

except in the physical; but the physical does not make the man complete. Man is part physical as well as part spiritual; the physical life we live here to our satisfaction, the spiritual life we give to God when He calls us. And how many of us in the world today, if called for the spiritual life, will give that life as spotless as Jesus by His example taught? When we look at the world today we think of sin, we think of injustice, of iniquity, a world where man because of his strength, because of his advantage abuses the rights of his brother.
When we look upon the oceans of injustice that are placed in the path of the weak, how much must we not realize the far distance that we are from God and the far distance that we are from the man Christ, who tried to teach us the life by which we should see salvation, the life that He came to redeem".

19. Christ's Doctrine Rejected by the Classes

"Christ brought a mission to the world. It was that of love to all mankind; that which taught man to love his brother, to be charitable, and when He taught that doctrine after He had assumed the form of manhood, what did the world do to Him? The world derided Him; the world scoffed at Him; they called Him all kinds of names. He was an impostor; He was a disturber of the public peace; He was not fit to be among good society; He was an outcast; He was a traitor to the king. That is what they said of Jesus when He went about teaching and preaching to men the way of salvation, pointing them to the light by which they would see their Heavenly Father. And even though He was the Son of God, even though He had power from on high, even though He worked miracles to prove that He was not only an ordinary man, they did not believe Him and they did not heed Him.

The very people among whom He was born, the very people whom probably He loved most were the people who cried out for the destruction and the death of this man, and even though He was the Christ, the Son of God, He could not save Himself from the dissatisfied rebels of His day and of His time. He went about Jerusalem, He went about the holy places, teaching the multitude; He appealed to the masses of the people to save them from their sins, and when the masses attempted to hear Him, when the masses indicated that they would follow Him, the classes who always rule said that he was a disturber of the peace. "We cannot allow this man to travel at large, disturbing the peace of the community. This man threatens the power of the state, therefore we must imprison Him. We must place Him out of the way so that He will not teach these people this new doctrine, the doctrine of love, the doctrine of human brotherhood and the doctrine of equality".

20. THE CHARACTER OF MAN

"Christ was the first great reformer. Christ did not go exclusively to the classes. He devoted His life to all; the classes rejected Him because He was not born of high birth, of high parentage, because He was not born in their immediate circle, He was not born of the physical blood royal, therefore they could not follow such a man—"His doctrine is unsound, and He is receiving the plaudits of the people; He is getting the sympathy of the crowd; can we allow it?" And the answer was no.

And even the Son of God—not man only, but the Son of God—was sought by the classes who have always held down the masses, because of His teaching for the spiritual glory (if not the physical) of the people whom He loved.
And so while we commemorate the birth of the Christ today, we must bear in mind the sufferings He underwent, the agony He underwent for the purpose of carrying out completely His mission,— the mission that brought Him down from heaven to earth. Christ came to save a sinful world; the world rejected him, and even at the last hour, after He had preached for years to the people; after He had aroused the suspicion and the curiosity of the masses of His time, when He was about to leave the world, He had not even twelve men who were honest enough to profess the faith; He had not made twelve faithful converts, and He was the Son of God. That proves to you the state of man's mind; that proves to you the character of man, and man has not changed much since Christ was here. If he has changed he has done so for the worse. And that brings me to the thought whether if Christ should come back to the world today in what way would He be received?
If Christ were to return to the world today, born in the same lowly state, born of the same humble parentage, and attempted to preach the same redemption, He would be imprisoned. He would be executed, He would be crucified in this twentieth century even as He was crucified nineteen hundred years ago on the Mount of Calvary. Man has not changed much".

21. CHRISTIANITY A MOVING FORCE

"But there is one lesson we can learn from the teachings of Christ. Even though man in the ages may be hard in heart and hard in soul, that which is righteous, that which is spiritually just, even though the physical man dies, the righteous cause is bound to live. Because the preaching of Jesus, the teaching of Jesus was not something physical; if it was something physical it would have died. The teaching of Jesus, the preaching of Jesus, was something spiritual, and where there is righteousness of spirit there is length of life. Jesus the man was not respected, Jesus the man was not adored, Jesus the man was not even loved by His own people, and for that they crucified Him; but the spiritual doctrines of Jesus were righteous; the doctrines of Jesus were just, and even though He died nearly nineteen hundred years ago, what has happened?
After the lapse of nineteen hundred years His religion is the greatest moving force in the world today, morally and spiritually. It shows you, therefore, the power of spiritual force; it shows you, therefore, the power of a righteous cause.

Jesus, who was the first great reformer, taught us the way; after Him followed the other great reformers who shared the same fate Born, perhaps, in the same lowly station of life, feeling with the masses of people who suffered like them, they have gone out, whether it be Luther or Saint Augustine or some other great reformer, but they have all gone out and they preached their doctrine, to suffer in their time for the doctrine to rise again on the wings of time and to flourish as the green bay tree".

MANKIND & CHRIST

22. MAN'S KINSHIP WITH HIS CREATOR

"Christmas symbolizes something other than the amusement that it affords today. Christmas brings us to the realization of the fact that hundreds of years ago, when man was practically lost in his spiritual kinship with his Creator and the world probably was to be wiped away, the Son of God Himself came down from His throne on high for the purpose of saving you and saving me.

We rejected Him in the past; our attitude now suggests no better consideration for Him if He should return, but with that patience, but with that love, but with that mercy, with that charity that caused Him to look down, not in revenge, but in the belief, in the hope, that some time man will change his ways—man will get to realize his true kinship with his Creator and be what his, God expected him to be.

But before we reach this point we need a better understanding of self, as individuals, and may I not appeal to the strong and mighty races and nations of the world for a better and a closer consideration and understanding of the teachings of the man Christ, who went about this world in His effort to redeem fallen man? May I not say to the strong, may I not say to the powerful, that until you change your ways there Will be no salvation, there will be no redemption, there will be no seeing God face to face? God is just, God is love, God is no respecter of persons; God does not uphold advantage and abuse to His own people; God created mankind to the same rights and privileges and the same opportunities, and before man can see his God, man will have to measure up in that love, in that brotherhood that He desired us to realize and know as taught to us by His Son Jesus.

Let us realize that we are our brother's keeper; let us realize that we are of one blood, created of one nation to worship God the common Father. It does not, therefore, suggest a proper understanding of our God or a proper knowledge of ourselves when in our strength we attempt to abuse and oppress the weak as is done to Negroes today".

23. THE SELFISHNESS OF MANKIND

"The statesmen of the world cry out for peace. They are meeting in many conferences with the hope that they will have peace; but I wonder if they understand the meaning of peace. There can be no peace until that peace reflects the spirit of the message of the angels of nineteen centuries ago. The real peace actuated by love, love as the Christ came to the world to give us; love for the high and mighty, love for the meek and lowly, love for all, is the only peace that will reign, is the only peace that will draw man nearer to his God. Man is so selfish that he does not seem to realize that there is anyone else in the world but himself.
The statesmen who lead America seem to believe that there is no one else in the world but the people who make up America, the statesmen who lead the British Empire (even though they cry for peace and desire peace) seem to believe that no one else lives in the World but men within the British Empire".

24. CHRIST IS FOR ALL, SO WE ARE FOR ALL

"Up to now we have not yet got the message of the angels; up to now they have not yet fully interpreted the spirit of Christ. Christ came into the world not to save one set of humanity, otherwise He would not have been the Christ. Christ came into the world to save mankind; therefore. His love must be for all; His love could not be sectional; His love could not be partial; His love was general and universal.
Therefore, before we can have peace on earth, before we can welcome the spirit of the high God; before we can get a true understanding of the spirit of the Christ, who came to us born in the lowly stable at Bethlehem, we must get to realize the brother- hood that exists, realize it in truth; realize it in fact, and practise it whether we be white, black or some other hue".

25. CHRIST TAUGHT LOVE

"The New Testament reveals the life of Christ as an exemplary one. His life was faultless to a word. Therefore, it is evident, that he must have been a superior creature.
If he had played the devil and behaved like the devil, there would have been no example to lead us to the perfection of God. Because his life was perfect, is evidence and fair assumption that he was the begotten Son of God. The greatest thing that Christ taught was love. Love thy neighbour as thyself; do unto others as you would have them do unto you. In these statements are wrapped the highest ideals of Godhead; as in the relationship of a father with his children. There has been no greater philosophy in the history of mankind. Support this philosophy and never change until God manifest himself to the contrary, which is not likely".

26. LET US LIVE LIKE CHRIST BOTH IN BODY AND SPIRIT

"...Realizing that Christ came to save all mankind from the fallen state, to restore man to his spiritual kinship with his God, let us practise a spirit of love, a spirit of charity, a spirit of mercy toward mankind; because in so doing we will be bringing God's kingdom down to earth. Let us live that true life, that perfect life in ourselves as spiritual beings, not forgetting that we are physical also; man must not fail to understand his dual personality. In being charitable and sympathetic like the Christ would have us to be does not mean to say that we must ignore our physical needs".

27. CHRIST NEVER CORRUPTED HIS SOUL

"It is evident that Christ had in his veins the blood of all mankind and belonged to no particular race. Christ was god in the perfect sense of his mind and soul. His spirit was truly God's spirit. His soul, which acted on the advice of God's spirit was never corrupt. Christ's soul was the free-will thought that is similar to the soul free-will thought of all men. Whilst other men with their free-will souls become corrupt and do evil even under the guidance of the Holy Spirit of God, Christ with his free-will soul never disobeyed the Holy Spirit guide of God".

28. God Not Interested in the Physical Activities of Man

"Christ was not so much interested in the physical responsibility of man; neither is God interested in the physical activities of man. That may be something strange to say at this hour when you have heard so much about religion. Christ cared so little for the physical that He offered Himself up and was satisfied to go on the cross and let the physical die. God the Father is interested in the spiritual of man, but man's physical body is for his own protection; is for his own purpose. Whatsoever you want to do with the physical God does not interfere, and I trust at this time when we are going to contemplate Christ that we will get a better understanding of Him and get a better understanding of the religion that He taught, because some of us seem to have some peculiar ideas about the religion of Jesus.

Some of us seem to believe that Christ and God the Father are responsible for all our ills—physical ills. They have nothing to do with our physical ills.

I repeat, God is not and Jesus is not interested in the bodies of men. If you want to care for your body, that is the privilege and prerogative given to you by God. If you want to destroy it, that is the same privilege and prerogative He has given. If you want to commit suicide, that is your business.

If you want to live, that is your business. God has given you the power; He has made you a free agent as far as the physical in life goes.

All that God is interested in is the spiritual; that you cannot kill, because the moment you destroy the physical body God lays claim to the spiritual with which you are endowed.

The spiritual Is never yours.. The spiritual is always God's, but the physical is your own property. If you want to break your physical life up, that is all your business. God does not interfere and that should be the Negro's interpretation in this twentieth century of Christ's religion. It is no use to blame God-and Christ for the things that happen to us in the physical; they are not responsible; they have absolutely nothing to do with it. If one man enjoys life and another does not, God has absolutely nothing to do with the difference between the two individuals. That is to say, if one man lives in a palace across the street and enjoys life and the other fellow lives in the gutter, God has nothing to do with the difference between them. It is purely a physical regulation left to man himself.

Make your interpretation of Christianity scientific—what it ought to be, and blame not God, blame not the white man for physical conditions for which we ourselves are responsible".

29. THE SPIRIT OF GOD AND THE MISSION OF CHRIST

"In every man there is the spirit of God, that is to say, that which is there to advise you and direct you to do good always. In each man also, is the free-will soul which is the mind. Each may accept the good guidance of the Holy Spirit or refuse to obey entirely.
Man generally disobeys the Holy Spirit of goodness and therefore becomes sinful. Christ never disobeyed the Holy Spirit of goodness, and that was why he was the Son of man with whom the spirit of God was well pleased because he lived a life so perfect as was intended when God made Adam and Eve.

The mission of Christ, therefore, was to redeem man from sin and place him back on the pinnacle of goodness as God intended when he made the first two creatures. The life of Christ is intended to show man that by obedience he can lift himself to the highest soul expression in keeping with the Holy Spirit of God, of which he is a part, but only with free-will. A free-will can do as he likes. Man has a body, a soul which is his own identification of himself and the Holy Spirit of God.

In the vilest man, there is the Holy Spirit of God and that man cannot destroy the Holy Spirit of God because that spirit in him is the unit of God which cannot sin and cannot die because it is everlasting goodness.

The thing that sins in man is the man's individual soul, which is his mind. When man corrupts this mind or soul, he is called bad. He is in rebellion against the Holy Spirit of God that is in him.

When he dies, as we know it and call it death; whether he dies a bad man or a good man, the Holy Spirit never dies, it goes right back to God, the everlasting goodness.

It is the soul of the man which identifies him as a unit of creation. That passes away if it is bad and lives on like Christ if it is good. You can judge the truth of this philosophy from your own experience. Try to remember how you think if it is not a fact that sometimes there is something in you that tells you do this, and another something at the same time tells you do that.

The Holy Spirit, which is goodness, is always telling you and advising you to do the right thing, but your free-will soul, which is mind, refuses to accept the instructions and advice of goodness.

There is always a debate with one's self to know what to do. You must analyze your system and your being so completely as to know when you are being advised by the Holy Spirit of goodness and follow that advice. If you can satisfactorily do that, then you can be like Christ and lift yourself to the highest plane of spirit and human life".

30. THE SIGN OF THE CROSS

"Man was redeemed by Christ to reach the perfect state as man, through his soul. The symbol of the Christ was the Cross in sentiment, therefore, man adores the Cross.

The Black man has a greater claim to the Cross than all other men. If it is a symbol of Christ's triumph, then the Negro should share in the triumph because Simon the Cyrenian bore the Cross. Simon the Cyrenian shared in the original triumph.

The shortest prayer we may give to God, even if we never pray otherwise, is to make the sign of the cross, and say at the same time, "In the name of the Father, the Son and the Holy Ghost."

It is a powerful prayer. It supersedes all others. If the words are repeated sincerely and earnestly from the heart. God answers that prayer. Do it always. In going to bed you need not make a long prayer. Make the sign of the Cross and repeat the words the Catholics do. The Catholics appreciate the value of the Cross. That is why they make the sign of the Cross as a part of their religion. But they have no right to the Cross because they crucified Christ on the Cross. The Cross is the heritage of the Black man. Don't give it up. This has nothing to do with the Roman Catholic religion. This is our religion and our interpretation of the significance of the Cross and Christ".

Garvey's Poem

Christ the Way

Oh, with the Spirit as of old,
I chant a prayer to my God;
The Being, precious,
more than gold
That Croesus has ever had.
I lift my soul to Him above,
And sing the angel's happy praise;
The song of life in joy of love
That men from earth to Heaven raise.
There's joy in Paradise for me,
Although a weary child of sin;
The penitent on Calvary's tree
May find the way to enter in.
My hopes are good, in Christ, the Lord;
On Him I rest my cares of heart;
He will so bridge the Heavenly Ford
To show the way ere I depart.
October 8, 1927

GARVEY'S PRAYER

MY ALTAR

I've built a sacred place all mine,
To worship God, who is Divine,
I go there every day, in thought,
Right to my own, dear sacred heart–

MY ALTAR
No one can change me in my mood,
For I do live on God's sweet food,
He feeds me every day, with love,
While angels look at it above–

MY ALTAR
When all the world goes wrong without,
I never hold one single doubt,
For I do find a great relief,
When I do trust my own belief–

MY ALTAR
I see the Saviour of the world,
Whose light to all has been unfurled,
He utters agonizing plea,
With shining eyes that surely see–

MY ALTAR
I shall remain with faith of rock
To see the Shepherd lead his flock,
And when He comes to claim each heart,
My yield shall be in wholesome part–

MY ALTAR

Made in the USA
Lexington, KY
29 January 2017